Opening up Thankfulness

At important times in the life of a family, school, religious community or nation we stop and express our thanks. Whether that is over the birth of a child or a celebration of sporting excellence, we celebrate, we reflect and we say thank you. That thankfulness might be expressed by standing on the street and applauding as athletes travel past in an open-top bus or with prayers, promises and a party saying thank you for the birth of a child.

This curriculum book explores a series of expressions of thankfulness that are relevant for 4–11 year olds. The units focus on how faith communities express gratitude and appreciation to God and how that affects the way people choose to live their lives.

The unit for 4–6 year olds uses some simple blessings from Judaism, embracing games, story, poetry and creativity. For 5–7 year olds we peep into thank you celebrations when a baby is born into a Christian, a Muslim and a Jewish family.

For older children we explore generosity as an expression of thankfulness through quotes from religious text, a story from the Bible and a contemporary website. The harvest festival is a part of many a school year; this unit expects children to work together in a series of interpretation, creative and judgement tasks around creating relevant and meaningful harvest celebrations. The final unit provides excellent stimulus material to enquire into remembrance celebrations, offering rich opportunities for cross-curricular linking with learning in History.

For the subject leader we have provided a set of pages to improve teachers' understanding of thankfulness, together with quotations from a selection of religions on this important human capacity.

Fiona Moss

Web links: RE Today website

The RE Today website offers subscribers some free additional resources and classroom-ready materials related to this publication. Look out for the 'RE Today on the web' logo at the end of selected articles.

To access resources:

- go to the RE Today website www.retoday.org.uk

- click on the **download login** button and use the password from this term's issue of *REtoday* magazine

- click on **Primary curriculum publication – web supplement**

- click on the title of the publication and scroll down the page to find what you are looking for.

RE Today
Services

WHY IS IT GOOD TO SAY THANK YOU?

For the teacher

Encouraging children to say thank you is an important part of their social, emotional and moral development.

This unit helps children aged 4–6 to explore and experience thanking and being thanked. It links to the Jewish practice of expressing gratitude and appreciation to God, as well as to the story of the Ten Lepers being healed by Jesus, where only one returned to say thank you. This can help children to reflect on ideas of right and wrong, good and bad actions.

It also connects with findings from psychology about the benefits of expressing gratitude. Research suggests that grateful people are calmer, happier, healthier, more optimistic, more empathic and less vulnerable to depression than ungrateful people. This shows the value of the Jewish practice of saying grateful blessings a hundred times a day!

Activity I

Thanks/no thanks game

Use this version of 'Pass the Parcel' to get children to say thank you, and also to experience what it is like not to be thanked.

Sit children in a circle and hand one child a special object, such as a teddy bear.

Play some music.

The child turns to his right and says, 'This is for you, [name]' and the second child says, 'Thank you, [name]'. The second child turns to child 3 and continues the thanking pattern.

Stop the music. When the music is off, the child passes the teddy on, with the same words – 'This is for you . . .' but this time the child who receives it does not say thank you. Continue a few goes, then turn the music back on. Children start to say thank you again.

Talk about how it feels to thank and be thanked, and about not thanking or being thanked.

What can children do as a result of this unit?

This article supports children working within the Early Learning goals outlined below, and the pupil friendly 'I can' statements for level 1 and 2 describe what older or more able pupils may achieve through this work.

Early Learning goals	These activities help young children to
	• **listen and attend:** listen to stories, give their attention to what others say and respond appropriately
	• **manage feelings and behaviour:** talk about how they and others show feelings, talk about their own and others' behaviour, and its consequences, and know that some behaviour is unacceptable
	• **make relationships:** show sensitivity to others' needs and feelings
	• **be imaginative:** represent their own ideas, thoughts and feelings through art, role-play and stories.
Level 1	I can . . . • recognise some Jewish thank-you blessings and recall the story of the person who said thank you to Jesus • *talk about what I am thankful for.*
Level 2	I can . . . • say why Jewish people might say thank you to God 100 times a day. • *talk about what is good about being thanked and being thankful.*

The following resources are available for subscribers to download from the RE Today website:

• A large version of the emoticon flash cards on page 6

See: www.retoday.org.uk/supplements

Activity 2

Jewish blessings or 'Thank you' prayers

Tell the children that many Jewish people say short prayers to God through the day. These short 'blessings' use the same sentence stem and can be used for hundreds of situations and experiences through the day. There are some examples on page 4.

Gather together some images to show on the whiteboard to illustrate the blessings. Read through the blessings on page 4, showing the picture and reading the text.

Ask the children:

- Why might Jewish people want to bless or thank God for these things?

Choose some more items or events from everyday life and ask your children what the Jewish prayer might be for that moment.

Activity 3

Being thankful poem

Using the Jewish practice of thanking God a hundred times a day as a starting point, ask your children to **talk together about** things they are thankful for.

It will be more appropriate in the classroom to get children to express this by saying 'I am thankful for . . .' rather than using the Jewish form of blessing to God.

Use the writing frame on page 5 to help children structure their own response.

Ask the children to:

- draw something in at least three boxes

- **describe** what they have drawn and **say why** they are thankful for this.

Has your class managed to be thankful for 100 things?!

Activity 4

A thank-you story

Tell the story of Jesus and the Ten Lepers from the Christian Bible (Luke 17:11-19), found on page 6.

Put the words with emoticons at the bottom of page 6 onto card and give one or two to each pair of children.

As you tell the story, if they think one of the characters has a matching feeling, they should hold up their card.

Ask the children:

- Who would feel like this and why?

Explain to the children that Jesus was Jewish and that the 10 ill men were Jewish too – so they really should know better about saying thank you!

Ask the children to act out:

- feeling ill

- being ignored by everybody

- getting better

- saying thank you to the person who helped you get better

Ask the children to imagine how Jesus would have felt about:

- the one who came back

- the nine who didn't.

Talk about whether they would have been the one or one of the nine.

- Do they always say thank you?

Activity 5

Thank-you bags

Being thankful is not something you can keep to yourself. Ask the children why not!

Ask the children to:

- think of someone they really want to say thank you to

- design and make their own thank-you bag. They could use the net and the boxes on page 7.

- draw or write something they want to thank that person for on paper

- cut it out and put it in the bag

- take it to the person, give it to them and say why they want to say thank you.

On-going gratitude is really important. Why not get children to practise being thankful each day – perhaps when you call the register?

Keep a 'Thank-you bag' pinned to the wall in your classroom for children to put their ideas in each week. Have a form saying *'I am thankful to . . . for . . . '*

Read the thank-you forms and distribute them each week.

Jewish blessings or 'Thank you' prayers

Many Jewish people use some short prayers called 'Baruch atah Adonai'. They are little statements that usually start with 'You are blessed, O Lord our God, king of the universe who ...' There are hundreds of them for every occasion. Here are some.

Eating apples or pears (that grow on trees)
'You are blessed, O Lord our God, king of the universe, who creates the fruit of the tree.'

Eating raspberries or strawberries (that grow on bushes from the ground)
'You are blessed, O Lord our God, king of the universe, who creates the fruit of the ground.'

Eating bread
'You are blessed, O Lord our God, king of the universe, who brings forth bread from the earth.'

On seeing mountains
'You are blessed, O Lord our God, king of the universe, who creates the wonders of the world.'

On seeing a rainbow
'You are blessed, O Lord our God, king of the universe, who keeps his covenant with humanity.' (Jewish people remember the story of Noah, where the rainbow was a sign that God would never again destroy the earth with a flood.)

On hearing thunder
'You are blessed, O Lord our God, king of the universe, whose power and might fill the universe.'

On seeing people with disabilities or unusual body shapes
'You are blessed, O Lord our God, king of the universe, who creates diversity in your creatures.'

On wearing new clothes or having new experiences
'You are blessed, O Lord our God, king of the universe, who has preserved me to live to this time.'

On seeing teachers or scholars
'You are blessed, O Lord our God, king of the universe, who has distributed his wisdom to humanity. '

Talk about these blessings with the pupils.

• Why do some Jewish people want to thank God like this?

A challenge
One special Jewish book, the Talmud, says that Jewish people should try to say thank you to God 100 times a day! Can your class come up with 100 things to be thankful for? If every member of the class thinks of five ... and if they are five different things ...

RE Today
Services

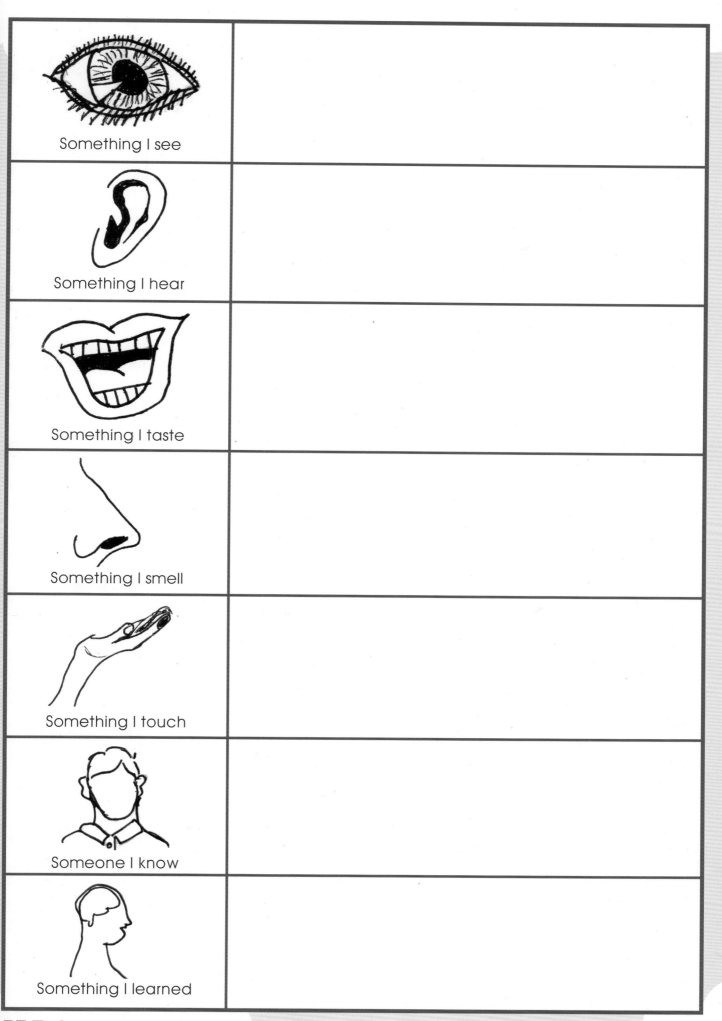

Something I see	
Something I hear	
Something I taste	
Something I smell	
Something I touch	
Someone I know	
Something I learned	

Saying thank you: a story

This is a famous Christian story, starring 11 Jewish men who would have known about being thankful.

Jesus was walking along the road with his friends. He could see a small village ahead. Outside the village there were ten men. They were ill with some painful skin diseases. Because their faces and arms looked so bad, and because they were ill, they were not allowed to join in with normal village feasts and events. They had to live outside the village.

They saw Jesus coming. They didn't come close to him but called from a distance. 'Jesus,' they called out. 'Master, have pity on us!'

Jesus looked at them and told them: 'Go and show yourselves to the priest.' He said this because it was only the priest who could say that they were allowed to come back and live in the village.

They did as Jesus said, and on their way to see the priest they got better! Their terrible skin diseases cleared up!

One of the men came from a nearby country – he was a Samaritan. When he saw that his skin was clean and that his pain had gone, he came back to find Jesus. He called out thanks to God in a loud voice.

When he saw Jesus, he fell on the floor at Jesus' feet and said thank you.

Jesus asked, 'Didn't all ten men get better? Where are the rest? Was it only this Samaritan who came to say thank you to God?' He helped the man get up and said, 'You can go now. Because you trusted God, you are healed.'

happy	sad	amazed	painful
upset	disappointed	excited	thankful
tired	lonely	hopeful	forgetful

THANK YOU

Thank you for . . .	Thank you for . . .	Thank you for . . .

HOW DO PEOPLE GIVE THANKS FOR A NEW BABY?

For the teacher

This section of the book explores a big experience: the arrival of a new baby. Pupils will learn that different communities give thanks for the arrival of a new baby in many different ways, but that there are some things similar in these celebrations and one of these is the feeling of thankfulness.

It's not surprising that all the world's religions mark new birth with a celebration of thanksgiving: feeling vulnerable, investing high hopes and wishing for much in the face of nature is central to the human experience of being new parents, and religious communities hallow and express these feelings.

Here you will find simple information and age-appropriate activities for 5–7s which refer to some practices in Muslim, Jewish and Christian communities.

Cross-curricular links

Geography

Pupils might find out about the country of Israel, where most people are Jewish, or a country such as Turkey or Egypt, where most people are Muslims. It's always good practice in RE to find out first about religion here, now – so begin with the local, and widen learning towards the national or global.

Literacy

Labelling and describing social practice contributes to pupils' use of spoken and written language.

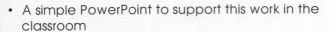

The following resources are available for subscribers to download from the RE Today website

- A simple PowerPoint to support this work in the classroom

See: www.retoday.org.uk/supplements

What can children do as a result of this unit?

The following pupil-friendly 'I can' statements describe the learning that may be expected of pupils in the 5–7 age range.

Level	Description of achievement: I can. . .
1	• **talk about** how babies are welcomed into the world by Christians, Muslims and Jewish people • ***talk about*** *belonging in their own lives: who do they belong to?* • **recall** some features of welcoming a baby in Islam, Judaism and Christianity.
2	• **retell** a story of a baby welcoming ceremony • **recall and suggest meanings** for some of the symbols associated with baptism, aqiqah and simchat bat. • ***respond sensitively*** *to ideas about how to welcome a new baby into the world, thinking for themselves.*
3	• **describe** two different ceremonies for welcoming a baby into a religion • list some **similarities and differences between** two baby-welcoming ceremonies • ***make simple links*** *to their own ideas from the religions they have learned about.*

See also

An excellent video clip of a Christian infant baptism:
See: www.cleo.net.uk

A useful slide show on dedicating a new baby in church:
See: www.request.org.uk/infants/milestones/baby/dedication03.php

An internet image search for the Muslim aqiqah ceremony can show your pupils a range of cards, photos and ideas about Muslim baby-welcoming.

RE Today
Services

Activity 1   Welcoming a baby

Ask the pupils if they can think of ways of making a new baby welcome to the world. This is a demanding task, so if they cannot come up with a list of ideas, it is good to offer some alternatives.

Ask them to choose and talk about baby-welcoming ideas in pairs (of course in practice these are not exclusive). What would be the best ways to welcome a new baby into the world? Would they rather . . .

- Get the baby some really beautiful clothes to wear, or buy the most expensive pram for the baby?
- Have a party for family and friends or take some photos for the baby to see when he or she grows up?
- Choose some special words to teach the baby or play some special music to the baby?
- Put some money in the bank for the baby or give some money to charity to say thank you for the safe arrival?

Teach the pupils that different religions have different ways of welcoming a new baby, and they are going to learn about two things that Muslims do to thank God for new babies. Ask them to talk in pairs about the examples: what makes these a good way of welcoming a baby?

Above: The first word a child hears is 'Allah'.

Below: Clipping the baby's hair.

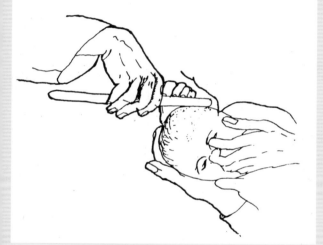

Activity 2   How do Muslims welcome a new baby?

Whispering important words

When a baby is born, Muslim dads whisper into the baby's ear. They whisper the most important words for Muslims. They whisper that there is no God but Allah, and the messenger of Allah is Muhammad.

The full Adhan (call to prayer) can be found at: www.islamcan.com/audio/adhan/index.shtml

These are the first words a baby hears, and give a good start in life for Muslims.

Ask the pupils

- What would you whisper into a baby's ear as a welcome to the world?

Ask pupils to whisper their ideas to each other, then to share the idea their partner gave with the class. Emphasise that these ideas are not going to be used by millions, like the Muslim words – but are still interesting.

A hair cut and a gift in silver

The second ritual for welcoming a baby into the Muslim community is that after one, two or three weeks of life, the baby will have his/her first haircut. Muslim parents like to weigh the hair: it might weigh just a few grams. It is a common custom to give the weight of the hair in silver to help poorer people. This is a sign of thanksgiving too: 'Thank you Allah for our beautiful new baby. We give this silver to show how grateful we are, and to help others who are not so fortunate.'

Ask the pupils to talk in pairs about an idea of their own that says 'thank you' for a new baby – would they give money, or silver, to a charity, or have they a different idea? Share and list all the ideas they come up with.

Many Waters

David's poem for Jack's Christian Baptism

Plop, plop, drip
The rain drops come down
Fresh spring showers
Clean all around

Trickle, trickle, gush
The stream flows on
Over rocks and sand
Hear the water run

Deep, deep, peace
The lake sits calm
The water lies still
Watch: see no harm

Break, break, crash
The water's in a rush
Waves are rolling in
Life makes a splash

Julia's Prayer for Baby Jack

Dear God

Thank you for giving us our lovely baby boy Jack.

Please help us to look after him.

While he is growing up, please take care of him and love him.

May he know Your peace and calm.

May his life be full of excitement.

Amen.

Activity 3   How do Christians say thank you for the birth of a baby?

Tell the class about a Christian christening or infant baptism. It is a way for the church community to join new parents in saying 'thank you' to God for the birth of a baby.

Give each pair a copy of the picture on page 11, with the three thought bubbles for the church minister, the mum and dad (Julia and David). Ask them to get ready to fill these thought bubbles up with their best guesses

- What do people think about at a christening?

Tell them that the baby's dad wrote a poem for this christening, all about water. The water at a christening is a symbol for many different things.

- What do they think water symbolises?

In the poem, water is a symbol for being clean and fresh, for gushing and rushing, for peace and calm and for making a splash.

Read and repeat the poem as a class, and ask pupils which verse they like best, and which lines connect up to the new baby's christening.

Tell them that Julia, the mum, wrote a prayer for her little boy as well.

Ask pupils which lines they like, and why.

Tell them that babies are usually given their names when they are baptised, and Julia and David's baby is called Jack.

All this may help them to fill in their thought bubbles in creative and interesting ways. Some pupils will write well in this structure. Others may be able to do three pictures and choose just a couple of key words. Make a class display of the finished pieces of work.

RE Today Services

Thankful

Grateful

Happy

Hopeful

Joyful

Loving

Water

Belonging

Baptism

David and Julia are Christians. They have come to bring their baby boy to be christened at their church. The baby's name is written down, and he is welcomed into the Christian community with water splashed on his head. He is given a candle to show that Jesus is the light of the world.

What are the people thinking?

A Jewish example: Miriam's new baby

My baby girl was born three weeks ago. We are a Jewish family, and I was so thankful to the Almighty for our lovely daughter. I asked the rabbi what we can do to welcome her into the world. He said that we should plan a simchat bat. It is a daughter's birth party. It's a day for being joyful.

So last Shabbat, after we went to synagogue, we had all our friends and family come home for a party. We had already named our little girl: she is called Sarah; but the Simchat Bat felt like her real naming.

We had the rabbi read a special part of our scriptures that say what a blessing a daughter is. In the olden days, there was a ceremony for little boys, but not for little girls. Today we gave thanks for our lovely girl!

We had a special prayer as well. It says:

'May the One who blessed our mothers and ancestors, Sarah and Rachel, Miriam and Esther, bless this beloved girl and her parents. Let her name be Sarah, and may she grow up with good health and peace. May her parents live to see her joy at her wedding and the birth of her own children, in prosperity and honour. Amen.'

I love this prayer so much I am going to have it written out to put on the wall in Sarah's bedroom!

RE Today
Services

Activity 4

Welcoming a Jewish baby girl

Tell the children the story of Miriam's baby on page 12. Show the children the black and white drawing of Miriam, her husband and the baby.

What else might the family be doing to celebrate her birth? How might they use the tallit and the Shabbat candles in the ceremony?

Activity 5

Being thankful for new baby – drawing the learning together

Remind pupils of all they have learned in these lessons. You might give them a quiz about all the different ideas they have learned to do with saying thank you for a new baby.

A team quiz is fun, and cements factual learning. Here are 15 questions to try out (they are quite hard – but pupils in teams can do them):

1 Can you name three different religions that say 'thank you' for new babies?

2 Which religion has a synagogue for its holy building?

3 Which religion's followers whisper important words into the new baby's right ear?

4 Which religion has a font full of water to welcome a new baby?

5 What is the Muslim word for God?

6 To help Muslims decide on a gift to say thank you for a new baby, what do they weigh?

7 What metal is given away by thankful Muslims?

8 What religion uses water to welcome a baby?

9 Which religion has a candle as part of its way of welcoming a new baby?

10 What is a simchat bat?

11 What does the water of baptism stand for or symbolise?

12 Which religion has a haircut as a part of its welcome for a new baby?

13 What is the Adhan?

14 Who is the Jewish leader who helped at the Simchat Bat?

15 What is another word for infant baptism?

Activity 6

A creative challenge for a group

Ask the pupils in small teams to think about the list of different things they learned that welcome a new baby:

- Choosing a name for the baby
- Getting the family together
- Whispering in the baby's ear
- Giving a gift to the poor
- Having a party
- A cake
- Reading out holy words
- Saying a prayer
- Writing a poem
- Choosing music for the baby

Ask the small teams to take the list, and draw and write about their five favourite ways of welcoming a baby and showing thankfulness. They might be asked to imagine their own variations on all these rituals and customs.

Enactments

Teachers might think about whether it would be good learning to enact the rituals we describe in this work with a doll to the class.

There are some issues here: a trite bit of doll play done too quickly is no help in building respect for diversity, but if this is carefully planned, and includes perhaps some dressing up in appropriate costume, and careful attention to the symbols and ideas used, then enacting how a Muslim, Jewish and Christian baby are welcomed, with a focus on giving thanks, could be really good learning.

WHY SHOULD RELIGIOUS PEOPLE LIVE GENEROUSLY?

For the teacher

This unit explores the way that religious believers are taught to show thankfulness for everything they believe God has provided for them by showing generosity in the way that they live.

Pupils are enabled to make links between religious teaching and behaviour of religious believers. Religion is about belief and behaviour. All too often it can be presented as a series of rules, but for believers it is about a guide to how they should make all sorts of life decisions including use of money, possessions and time.

Using a series of quotes from religious text, a story from the Bible and a contemporary website, these activities enable pupils to:

- explore the impact of religious beliefs on the way people live their lives

- reflect on their own beliefs, values perceptions and experiences in the light of their learning.

Curriculum links

These activities make a contribution to the spiritual, moral, social and cultural development (SMSCD) of pupils:

- **spiritually** by learning about and reflecting on a story from the Bible and quotes from sacred text on the practice of generosity

- **morally** by considering how religious beliefs have an impact on people's actions

- **socially** by considering the impact individual and collective generous actions have on society.

What can children do as a result of this unit?

The following pupil-friendly 'I can' statements describe the learning that may be expected of pupils in the 7–11 age range.

Level	Description of achievement: I can. . .
2	• **identify** two good reasons to practise generosity • *respond sensitively to the idea of generosity.*
3	• **describe** religious beliefs about generosity and say how these are put into practice by believers • *ask some questions of my own about generosity in the world today and suggest two different answers to the questions.*
4	• **describe** how the beliefs of two religions about generosity might have an impact on the way someone lives his or her life • *express my own ideas about generosity, referring to two ideas from religions or beliefs I have studied.*

RE Today
Services

Activity 1

What do religions say?

This activity helps pupils to make links between religious teaching and behaviour of religious believers. Religion is about belief and behaviour.

Arrange pupils to work in pairs. Give each pair a set of the quotes from the top half of page 16.

Ask pupils to

- **read** each quote aloud to one another
- **explain** what they think it means
- **give an example** of what action a religious believer might do to act on the advice in the quote.

Give each pair a cut-up copy of the quotes from the bottom half of page 16.

Ask pupils to:

- **read** the quotes from each of the children
- **match** each child's quote to one of the religious quotes. Which action could be a result of following the advice in the religious quote? Could any of the children's quotes be linked to more than one of the religious quotes?

Activity 2

Living generously: what does it mean?

Show the pupils the Living Generously website.

See: www.generous.org.uk/actions

Arrange the pupils to work in pairs.

Ask the pupils to:

- **look** at the website. Choose a category and read five of the actions suggested.
- **consider** whether they would be able to do the actions
- **choose five actions** and give each a **mark out of 10** according to how difficult the action would be for them to carry out (1= easy, 10= difficult)
- **consider the impact:** for the same five actions, give a mark out of 10 according the impact that carrying out the action would cause (1 = not much impact, 10 = a lot of impact).

Action	How difficult?	How much impact?
Stop using plastic bags at the supermarket	2/10	7/10

Activity 3

Small steps make a big change

The strapline on the Living Generously website says

Small Steps Taken Often by Many People Mean Big Changes for the Planet and All the People who Live Here.

Give each pupil a copy of the diagram on page 17.

Ask the pupils to:

- **choose a generous action** and draw a picture of it being carried out in the rectangle at the bottom of the diagram. Write a short description under the picture.
- **show impact:** draw an arrow from the action showing how far the action will have an impact. Write about what the impact is in any of the relevant circles. For example, a picture of someone only using one car instead of two would stretch to the world. The sentence written in the world circle could say

  World – less oil used causes less pollution

  Community – roads less busy and safer

  Me – walk more so healthier.

Activity 4

What can Christians learn from a Bible story?

Read the pupils the story of the Ten Lepers from the Bible (Luke 17: 11-19). A version of this can be found on page 6.

Arrange the pupils to work in groups.

Ask the pupils to:

- **create a dramatic presentation** of the story suitable for use as part of a church service. Make sure the dramatic retelling shows what Christians can learn from the story.
- **write a paragraph for the vicar,** minister or priest to use in a sermon explaining to Christians what actions they might do to show how thankful they are for what God has given them.

Anyone who has two shirts should share with the one who has none, and anyone who has food should do the same.

Bible, Luke 3: 11

Those who act kindly in the world will have kindness.

Qur'an 2.172

What sort of religion can it be without compassion? You need to show compassion to all living beings.

Compassion is the route of all religious faiths

Hindu Basavanna Vacana 247

Every third year give a tenth of your crops to the foreigners, the orphans and the widows so that everyone in the community will have all they need to eat.

Torah and Bible, Deuteronomy 26: 12

O you who believe! Eat of the good things that we have provided for you and be grateful to God, if it is Him that you worship.

Qur'an 2.172

A man is worth many sparrows, but not one sparrow can die unnoticed in God's world.

Bible, Matthew 10:29

We used to have two cars but now we only have one car and Dad cycles to work.

Levi, age 9

We only eat free range eggs – we don't like the idea that chickens don't get to go outside.

Jessica, age 7

When we get our spending money we always put 50p in the charity pot. We use that money when we want to support charities like Children in Need.

George, age 8

We always say a sort of thank-you prayer before we eat. Dad says it helps us to remember how hard people have worked for the food.

Anish, age 9

Even though Fairtrade things cost more, we buy them when we can because it means that people who grow the cotton and cocoa and make the clothes and chocolate get paid enough.

Fatima, age 11

When it was my mum's birthday she told everyone she didn't want presents but she wanted people to buy things from Christian Aid for people in countries abroad. I bought some pencils and a book for a child in Uganda

Sara, age 10

RE Today
Services

Activity 3 Small steps make a big change

Enlarge this page to A3.

The world

Your town or village

Family and friends

You

Your action:

1 Draw a picture of your idea for a generous action in the rectangle at the bottom of the page.

2 Draw an arrow showing how far the impact of your action will stretch.

3 Write a sentence underneath your picture to explain your generous action.

4 Write a description of the impact in one or two of the circles.

RE Today Services

WHY DO CHRISTIANS CELEBRATE HARVEST?

For the teacher

A celebration of the harvest has been happening in Britain for over a thousand years. It is celebrated after the harvest has been gathered in to show that people are grateful for the food that has been grown. In Britain, harvest celebrations happen in September or early October.

Celebration of the Harvest Festival in church began in 1843 in Cornwall and throughout Victorian times harvest hymns such as 'All things bright and beautiful' were written.

Thanksgiving for harvest happens all over the world and in many religions: e.g. Judaism (Sukkot), Hinduism (Holi) and Sikhism (Baisakhi).

This work is designed to enable pupils 7–9 to think about:

- the meaning of the celebration of harvest
- the purpose and relevance of this celebration in the twenty-first century
- the purpose and relevance of this celebration to town and country.

This work is set up with an imaginary vicar or minister to allow pupils to take part in judgement tasks on the suitability of different hymns for celebrations and different charities for donations at different schools and churches. It would be even better if you could replace Reverend Bob with your local vicar or minister.

Description of Reverend Bob

Reverend Bob has just moved to a new church in the city centre called St Matthew's. It is a busy church with lots of families and children as well as older people. He used to be the vicar of a small village church in the middle of a farming community. He loves visiting schools and regularly visits them to take assembly and see the pupils. He visited Mid City Primary School last week.

What can children do as a result of this unit?

The following pupil-friendly 'I can' statements describe the learning that may be expected of pupils in the 7–9 age range.

Level	Description of achievement: I can. . .
2	• **identify two simple reasons** why Christians celebrate Harvest Festival • ***talk about*** *thanksgiving for food, and give reasons why it matters.*
3	• **make a link** between the Christian celebration of harvest and the words of harvest hymns • **use appropriate religious vocabulary** for Christian harvest celebrations • ***suggest answers*** *that Christians might give to questions about the importance of thanksgiving and harvest.*
4	• **describe and link up** Christian harvest charities and actions and Christian beliefs about thanksgiving • ***suggest reasons***, *using examples, why a community might choose to support a particular harvest charity.*

The following resources are available for subscribers to download from the RE Today website:

- The answers to the tangled hymns activity on page 21
- The emails from Reverend Bob on page 20
- The charity description cards page 23
- The location description cards page 24.

See: www.retoday.org.uk/supplements

RE Today Services

Activity 1
What is Harvest Festival?

Introduce the Christian festival of Harvest to the pupils. Ask them to collect or 'harvest' what they know under a series of headings:

When?

Why?

What?

Who?

Once the class has collected together their knowledge, ask children to identify a series of questions that they have about harvest. Prioritise the questions and choose 5 or 6 questions for the class to investigate.

Give a question to each group and ask them to collect information from a variety of sources, e.g.

- The school library
- The local church
- The internet:

  Email a believer – see: http://pof.reonline. org.uk/emailproject/index.php

  REQuest – see: www.request.org.uk/main/ festivals/harvest/harvest01.htm

  Send a Cow – see: www.sendacow.org.uk/ harvest-festival

  BBC Class clips –clip 4466: see: www.bbc. co.uk/learning zone/clips/

Add to the knowledge gathering you did at the beginning of the lesson. Have the pupils been able to answer all their questions?

Activity 2
Tangled harvest hymns

Now that pupils have gathered lots of knowledge about harvest, explain that they are going to need to put it to the test.

Introduce the fictional vicar, Reverend Bob. Read the description of Reverend Bob on page 18. Explain that they need to imagine that he came to visit their school last week and that he has emailed them a series of challenges.

Read 'Email A' on page 20, and discuss with the class the challenges they have been set.

1. Explain that the words to the two hymns that Reverend Bob has sent have got tangled up so their first task is to untangle the words. Give them a copy of the tangled hymns on page 21.

   - Ask the pupils to work in pairs to separate the two hymns.
   - Ask them to underline 'Harvest Hymn' in one colour and 'We Plough the Fields and Scatter' in another colour.

2. Give each pair a copy of the untangled hymns. These can be found at the web links below. You may want to select just the first two or three verses that are used in the tangled hymn activity for the pupils to work with. Read through the words with the pupils, and ask them to:

   - as a pair, choose which they think is the best for a Harvest Festival celebration in a city primary school
   - as a class, come up with reasons for using each of the hymns
   - as a class, take a vote to choose the best hymn for the school Harvest Festival celebration.

   See: www.stainer.co.uk/hymns/harvest2.html

   See: www.hymns.me.uk/we-plough-the-fields and scatter-hymn.htm

Activity 3
Writing a modern harvest song

The second challenge set by Reverend Bob is to write a modern harvest hymn.

Ask the pupils to suggest words and phrases related to harvest. Remind the pupils it is a song for Christian children to sing in church. What Christian ideas does it need to include?

Give the pupils a stripped-down version of 'We Plough the Fields and Scatter' as a framework for their song.

We . . .
The . . .
But . . .
By God's . . .
He sends . . .
The . . .
The . . .
And . . .

Chorus

All . . .
Are . . .
Then thank . . .
O Thank . . .
For . . .

Email A

| New | Send | Delete | View | Help |

From: RevBob@stmatthewschurch.org.uk

To: class4@midcityprimary.sch.uk

Hi

It was great to meet you for the first time last week - you were all so friendly. St Matthew's Church and Mid City Primary are so different from the small village where I used to be vicar. The school only had 30 children in it!

I have started thinking about what you said about the church and school not doing anything about harvest, as you think it doesn't really have anything to do with people who live in a city.

I think you are wrong, so I have a challenge for you. Will you work with me to create a harvest celebration for rest of the school?

The first part of the challenge is below. I have sent two songs that we could use — 'Harvest Hymn' is a modern hymn and 'We Plough the Fields and Scatter' is a traditional hymn. Which do you think is better? Will you also think about writing some words for a harvest song of your own that would be suitable for me to get the children at St Matthew's to sing?

Bye

Reverend Bob

Email B

| New | Send | Delete | View | Help |

From: RevBob@stmatthewschurch.org.uk

To: class4@midcityprimary.sch.uk

Hi

I'm really sorry there was such a mess-up with the last email but I'm glad you managed to sort out the two hymns. They are very different, but as you point out, each has their good points and things that make them worth singing at harvest time in the 21st century.

The children in my groups at church loved the song you wrote for them and have even made up actions and play percussion instruments when they sing. I am going to upload a clip so you can watch them perform.

Now we have decided that we are going to have a harvest celebration in the church and in your school, I have a new challenge!

In the attachment I have sent details of four ways we might use the donations that people bring to the harvest celebrations at St Matthew's Church, my old village church, your school and the school in my old village. Can you work in groups and put together some ideas about which will be best? I'll pop into school next week to listen to your ideas.

Bye

Reverend Bob

RE Today
Services

Tangled Hymns

The two hymns that Reverend Bob has sent for you to think about using in your Harvest Festival celebration have got all tangled up in the email.

Can you identify which lines come from the modern urban hymn and which come from the older more rural hymn?

Now join we, to praise the Creator,

our voices in worship and song;

we stand to recall with thanksgiving

We plough the fields and scatter

The good seed on the land,

But it is fed and watered

By God's almighty hand:

that to God all seasons belong:

He sends the snow in winter,

We thank you, O Source of all goodness,

for the joy and abundance of crops,

The warmth to swell the grain,

The breezes and the sunshine,

And soft, refreshing rain.

for food that is stored in our larders,

for all we can buy in the shops.

All good gifts around us

Are sent from heaven above;

But also of need and starvation

we sing with concern and despair,

Then thank the Lord,

of skills that are used for destruction,

O thank the Lord,

of land that is burnt and laid bare.

For all his love.

Then teach us, O God of the harvest,

to be humble in all that we claim,

to share what we have with the nations,

to care for the world in your name.

He only is the maker

Of all things near and far;

He paints the wayside flower,

He lights the evening star;

The winds and waves obey him,

By him the birds are fed;

Much more to us, his children,

He gives our daily bread.

RE Today Services

Activity 4
Harvest donations – a judgement task

Read the pupils 'Email B' on page 20 from Reverend Bob. Spend time discussing with the pupils what they have been asked to do.

Arrange the pupils into either four or eight groups and give each group one of the cards on page 23 to work with.

Understanding

Each group needs to read through their card and discuss exactly what the charity they are looking at does. Ask the pupils to draw a poster that could be used to collect harvest donations for this charity.

The poster must show:

- what people need to bring to a harvest celebration
- what their donation will be used for
- a picture that is eye-catching and relevant.

Each group then needs to present their poster to the rest of the class.

Judgement

Give each of the groups a full set of the charity cards on page 23.

Ask each group to act on behalf of one of the four locations. Give each group a card from page 24 outlining the details of their location:

- St Matthew's
- Mid City Primary School
- Reverend Bob's old village church
- St Luke's C of E Primary School – the village school.

Each group has to read through the details of each charity and:

- rank the charities from most suitable to least suitable for their location to donate to
- choose which charity their location will collect harvest donations for
- record their choice using the sentence starter below.

   The best harvest charity for . . . . is . . . because . . .

Persuasion

Ask the pupils to work in their groups to prepare a one-minute presentation to show to Reverend Bob. The presentation must show:

- which charity has been chosen for this location
- why this charity is the best harvest charity for this location.

Persuade someone to role-play the part of Reverend Bob to listen to the presentations. Better still, persuade the local vicar/minister to come in and listen.

Salvation Army volunteer sorting through donated food to be given as food parcels.

RE Today
Services

The Salvation Army

The **Salvation Army** is a Christian group that collects food to give out in parcels to those who need them in your local area, e.g. people who have lost their jobs, or are ill or who cannot afford to feed their families.

We will collect tinned and dried food as we keep it at our food bank and give donations to people when they ask for help.

Why not bring dried or tinned food along to your harvest celebration. We will visit your celebration and explain how we help people in your area with the food you have donated.

See: www.salvationarmy.org.uk

Grow your Own

Support a local project where volunteers are working with unemployed people teaching them to grow their own food in the local allotments.

As well as learning an important skill that they will be able to use in other plots on the allotment, members of the group are learning to grow healthy food that they can harvest themselves.

Bring donations of vegetable seeds or money donations so we can buy seeds and tools.

Send a Cow — Change a family's future

The charity **Send a Cow** raises money to support families in Africa by, for example, buying them a cow, goat or chickens and providing training in animal care. An animal provides a gift that continues to feed a family through milk or eggs, and even the manure can be used to help crops grow.

If your community raises just £20 four chickens can be given to a family to provide fresh eggs. Twelve fruit trees can be provided for a family for £33.

Instead of bringing produce to your harvest celebration, bring a donation for Send a Cow. Alternatively, use some of the fundraising activities on our schools website at

See: www.sendacow.org.uk
See: www.cowforce.com

Harvest Where You Live

How many people do you know on your street? Do you know the elderly people who live near your home, church or school?

Keep up the harvest tradition and personally deliver a box of food to one of the elderly people in your community.

A box containing some fresh and tinned goods and maybe even a homemade cake will really cheer someone up who lives just around the corner in your community.

St Matthew's Church

Reverend Bob's city-centre church. A busy church with lots of families and young people who work in the city. In the congregation there are also some older, retired people who live near the church.

Mid City Primary School

A large primary school with over 400 pupils. The school is a community school in the middle of a housing estate in the city. Families in the school come from all around the world. Some of the parents work in the local hospital, others work in shops in the city and some others are unemployed.

St Luke's C of E Primary School – the village school

A small school of only 30 children. All the children live in the village or on local farms. Some people work on the farms but others travel a long way to find work.

Revd Bob's old village church

A small church that always holds a Harvest Festival. A group of people from the village come and decorate the church with fresh vegetables and wheat from the fields.

Activity 5
A report in the parish newsletter

Ask the pupils to write a short report that is suitable to go in the church newsletter. Note:

- the audience for the report is the members of St Matthew's Church
- the purpose of the report is to show what the children understand about Harvest Festival and the harvest charities that donations can be collected for.

Offer pupils a series of sentence starters.

Harvest is about . . .

It is important in the city as well as the country because . . .

Or

It is less important in the city because . . .

The charity . . . is suitable for donations in . . . because . . .

Hi Class 4

Brilliant Harvest celebration! Really sorry but I had to dash off.

Loved hearing about why you had chosen what to collect donations for. Do you think you could write a short report for the church newsletter explaining what you have learnt about Harvest Festival?

Thanks

Bob

RE Today
Services

WHY IS IT IMPORTANT TO REMEMBER THOSE WHO FIGHT IN WAR?

For the teacher

There is a profound dimension to **thankfulness** which can be explored through a consideration of the way in which we **remember** those who have been called upon – or who have volunteered – to fight in the armed forces in times of conflict.

This section provides four pages of stimulus material to help engage pupils and stimulate learning. The pages are a flexible resource, and can be used independently of the activities suggested.

Pages 26 and 27 present some unique insights into what it meant for a young man to be called up into the army in 1943, through extracts from the letters and artwork he sent home to his parents. Some questions to think about, suitable for individuals or small groups, are provided.

Pages 28 and 29 take a wider and more eclectic look at some significant events that are part of our national history, which say something about what and how we remember, and how we are thankful to those who are prepared to defend their country in times of war. Some questions to think about, suitable for individuals or small groups, are provided,.

Page 30 outlines three activities, drawing on the stimulus material on pages 26–29. They encourage questioning, finding out, discussion, understanding a variety of perspectives, and opportunities for reflection and expressing own views. Access to the internet is helpful, with video stimulus providing additional and relevant information and comment.

Curriculum links

This unit links to teaching in History in the unit 'Britain since 1930' often taught to 9–11s. This supports pupils' learning and skills in historical enquiry, allowing them to:

* pursue investigations to find answers to historical questions
* use sources to establish evidence for particular enquiries
* present and structure their findings in a variety of ways.

What can children do as a result of this unit?

The following pupil-friendly 'I can' statements describe the learning that may be expected of pupils in the 9–11 age range.

Level	Description of achievement: I can. . .
3	• **describe** what some people from one religion I have studied believe about peace and conflict and how this belief influences how they behave
	• *compare* some of the beliefs about peace and conflict that are important to me with those that influence believers from one of the religions I have studied.
4	• **show that I understand** some of the ways in which serving in the forces had an impact on the faith of those who took part
	• *express* my own questions and views about peace and conflict and suggest why it is sometimes difficult to live these out in practice.
5	• **suggest reasons** why people from one religion I have studied might hold differing views about war
	• *express* my own views on questions about peace and conflict, taking account of ideas from one of the religions I have studied.

See also
A Sense of Place

This DVD and CD-ROM presents video clips, an extensive collection of photographs and some classroom activities. The pack is designed to support RE with 14–16s, with pupils themselves providing the commentary and their own reflections. However, with the exception of the activities, this resource provides a very valuable bank of stimulus materials for work with 9–11s.

The pack was designed and created by Emma Senior, RE Consultant (Staffordshire LA).

See: http://shop.retoday.org.uk/120304

Private James Derek Goss (1924–1992)

James Derek Goss was born in Nottingham on 25 July 1924.

Derek, as he was known, was called up into the army in March 1943 during the Second World War, at the age of 18. He trained as a signalman and served in India, Burma, North Africa and South Africa. He was discharged from the army in September 1947. He married in 1953 and had two children.

Derek was brought up as a Christian. He greatly valued the support given by his local church to soldiers and their families.

Following his death from cancer in 1992 his family found 90 airmail letters which Derek had written to his parents while he was in the army. Extracts from some of these letters, and some of the paintings he included in them, are shown here.

Letter 1

'A' Company
1st Batt East Yorks
c/o India Command

August 24th

Dear Mam, Dad and Rosemary

Talking serious, I've still had no mail. I miss your letters more than I care to say. I don't know how you are, or anything. It's one of the things that keeps me going. I suppose it's somewhere about, so cheerio, chins up.

Letter 2

14556207 JD Goss
'D' Company
1st Batt East Yorks
c/o India Command
Oct 29

Dear Mam, Dad and Rosemary

Just a few lines to let you know I am going on all right, and I hope you are all the same. I have been waiting anxiously for a letter to hear how Rosemary and the baby are getting on. I feel rather puffed up to know that I've got another niece. It's rather strange not knowing her name or anything. I hope I soon get a letter.

I hope by this time you have heard from Bill. It's rotten luck to have no news from him at this time. I can imagine how Rosemary feels, though Bill must be feeling a lot worse. I know he wouldn't have missed being home for anything in the world.

Note: Rosemary was Derek's older sister (born 1919).
Bill was Rosemary's husband. He was in the army, often out of contact with his family, and at one point held in a Japanese prisoner of war camp.

Painting on an airmail letter from India, 29 August

Letter 4

14556207 JD Goss
West Yorkshire Regt
BBBC Deolali North
India Command

Dear Mam and Dad

It is alright to let Roy have my bicycle – it will be rusted up if you don't, besides it would only disappoint him, but I would just like to mention that I do not want anything else giving away, stamps etc.

Letter 3

'A' Company
1st Batt East Yorks
c/o India Command
August 8th

Dear Mam and Dad

How is dad getting on with rabbit keeping? I hope he has still got some, and it's not long before I'm mucking them out again. What a day when I see you all again. It's a year this month since I was home – it seems like 50. Well, we have to take things as they come, and I'll have to close. Give my love to Rosemary. Cheerio.

Keep your spirits up.

RE Today Services

© 2013 RE Today Services
Permission is granted to photocopy this page for use in classroom activities in schools that have purchased this publication.

14556207 JD Goss   Letter 5
West Yorkshire Regt
No4 Company 2 Wing GHQU1
BBBC Deolali North
India Command
11 March

Dear Mam and Dad

Don't get down-hearted when the lads come home on leave. One of these days I will be coming and then we will have a real bust up. Until I do, keep smiling – it won't go on forever.

I don't suppose there are many young people left in Bagnall now. Has Gilbert Smith heard any more about being called up?

Painting on an airmail letter
sent from India 4 July 1944

14556207 JD Goss   Letter 6
'D' Company
12th Sherwood Foresters

Dear Mam, Dad and Rosemary
When I come home I'll see that neither of you go short of anything. There is one thing I thank the army for – it's made a man of me, and also it makes you value money. I can't tell you how much I think of you for doing without so that I could keep at the stores. There is one thing when I come home – I will be on full money and also have a nest egg with what you are saving, but remember if ever you are short you can always have mine.
They say that absence makes the heart grow fonder. It's true in every word. I miss you in a thousand ways but I just keep smiling. It can't go one for ever, and I'll be seeing you before long.

Nottingham
Letter 7

June 7th 1944

Dear Derek

Here we are again for the third time round with another little reminder that your old friends and acquaintances at Cinderhill Church have not forgotten you. We all hope and trust that you are well in health (if not wealth) and that the time is not far distant when your roving commission days in uniform are gone.

With every good wish for your welfare and happiness.

Yours sincerely

Frances M Cooke (Miss)

14556207 JD Goss   Letter 8
'D' Company
12th Sherwood Foresters
India Command
4th July 1944

Dear Mam and Dad

As you can see I have enclosed another drawing for your collection. I would like you to save them for me. I hope you like them. Don't think I do it to fill the space. I just want you to see some of the things I have seen.

To think about

1 **Read letters 1 to 8.** What do you think Derek

   a missed most about being away from home?
   b missed out on?

2 **Derek made sure** that he took his paints and paintbrushes with him. His letters often asked his 'Mam' to send him new ones. If you were conscripted into the army, what would you make sure you took with you? Why?

3 **Derek was fortunate** in coming home uninjured from the war. He walked back into his old job, got married and had a family.

   c What sacrifices do you think he, and his family, made?
   d How do you think he might have benefited from his time in the army?

RE Today
Services

Resource 1

© Emma Jardine

Memorial, National Memorial Arboretum

Resource 2

National Memorial Arboretum

The National Memorial Arboretum in Staffordshire was created in 1977 as a national place of remembrance of those who gave their lives in the service of their country, or suffered as a result of conflict, or whose lives make it fitting that they be remembered here.

There are more than 200 memorials in 150 acres of woodland, with new ones being added all the time. People from many religions and cultures are remembered here.

The Armed Forces Memorial commemorates those who have been killed on duty or as a result of terrorism from the end of the Second World War to current conflicts, e.g. Afghanistan.

There is a daily Act of Remembrance, including a moment of silence, in the Millennium Chapel. Visitors are encouraged.

See: www.thenma.org.uk

Resource 3

What is remembering?

Remembering . . .

is more than memories

is more than just saying 'thank you'

is not enough, but is something

helps the lessons of the past inform the actions of today

celebrates courage, honour, bravery, sacrifice, generosity and love.

Resource 4

A Widow's Story

We'd only been married for almost two weeks when Iain went off to the Falklands.

Seeing Iain off to the Falklands war was the hardest thing I've ever had to do – neither of us could have known we'd never see each other again.

On 21 May 1982, five ships were hit. One of them was the HMS Argonaut, Iain's ship. When I was told that Iain was "missing presumed dead" a part of me didn't want to believe it. There were five Iains on that ship; they might have got it wrong.

Iain's body never came home, so the Armed Forces memorial is a place where I can run my fingers over his name and be with him. My first visit was wonderful, but heart-breaking too. I stood there and talked to him for ages.

Widow of Able Seaman Iain M. Boldy

© Emma Jardine

Resource 5

© Emma Jardine

Poppies, National Memorial Arboretum

RE Today Services

How and why do we remember them?

© Lewis Whyld/Press Association Images

Gurkha Justice Campaign

On 21 May 2009 the Home Secretary announced that all Gurkha veterans who retired before 1997 with at least four years' service would be allowed to settle in the UK if they wish. This victory followed a long campaign headed by the actress Joanna Lumley. Since 1815 the Brigade of Gurkhas has fought for the British Crown in conflicts around the world. Gurkhas come from Nepal and are usually from Hindu or Buddhist backgrounds.

Resource 8

Some things that religions say about peace and conflict

1 Buddhism
He who destroys life … he digs up the very roots of his life.
Dhammapada 346

2 Christianity
Blessed are the peacemakers for they will be called the children of God.
Christian Bible, Matthew 5:9

3 Hinduism
Ahimsa, non-violence, comes from strength, and the strength is from God, not man. Ahimsa always comes from within.
Mahatma Gandhi

4 Islam
Do not take life – which Allah has made sacred – except for a just cause.
Qur'an, 17:33

5 Judaism
They shall beat their swords into ploughshares and their spears into pruning hooks; nation shall not lift up sword against nation.
Hebrew Bible, Isaiah, 2: 4

6 Sikhism
When all efforts to restore peace prove useless and no words avail, lawful is the flash of steel. It is right to draw the sword.
Guru Gobind Singh

See: www.bbc.co.uk/ethics/war

Resource 7

Remembrance Day at the Cenotaph, Whitehall

Remembrance Day is always the second Sunday of November and there is a service at the Cenotaph in London. The monarch lays a wreath and other tributes, dedicated to all who have suffered or died in war, are placed on the Cenotaph. Great care is taken to ensure that everyone is included.

Members of the Cabinet, opposition party leaders, former prime ministers and certain other ministers and the mayor of London are invited to attend the ceremony, along with representatives of the armed forces, merchant air and navy and fishing fleets, and members of faith communities. High Commissioners from Commonwealth countries also attend and lay wreaths.

See video of the ceremony: http://bit.ly/McNPHS

© Mark Cuthbert/UK Press/Press Association Images

Queen Elizabeth II laying a wreath at the Cenotaph

To think about:

1 **Look closely at Resource 1.** What do you think the sculptor is saying about the impact of war, and the importance of peace?

2 **Watch the video for Resource 7.** What does the music, colour, pace, people, and use of silence say to you about the nature and importance of this annual event?

3 **What do the religions** you have been studying this term say about war? What questions do you have? What are your own thoughts?

4 **If you were to write a poem** called 'Remembering' or 'Thankfulnesss' what would you write? Use Resources 1–7 to help you.

Activities

Activity 1
Reflecting on one soldier's experience

1 **Working in groups**, provide pupils with copies of the stimulus material on pages 26–27 about Private James Derek Goss.

   Ask pupils to answer the question 'What mattered most to Derek?' They could express their thoughts on a target board (four concentric circles with 'Matters most' in the centre, then 'Matters a lot', 'Matters a bit' and 'Doesn't matter'). They should give reasons for their choices.

2 **Tell pupils** that after the war the four medals he was entitled to were posted to him in a small box. Derek left the box unopened, and he never spoke to his family about his time in the army.

   Ask pupils to suggest why he may have done this – and to consider whether they need to make any changes to their answers to task 1.

3 **Tell pupils** that after the war Derek was married in church, encouraged his children to go to church with their grandparents, and was proud that one of them became an RE teacher. However, he no longer had much personal interest in the religion of his birth.

   Ask pupils to suggest why they think his attitude to religion changed. What questions do you think he had? What answers might pupils suggest to these questions?

Activity 3
Visiting a memorial site

Enable pupils to visit a place where those who died in war are remembered. This might be:

- A cenotaph or other public memorial close to the school
- A memorial in a local place of worship
- The Cenotaph, Whitehall, London
- The National Memorial Arboretum, Staffordshire.

If a visit is not possible, then explore with pupils the videos on the weblinks identified on pages 28–29. The DVD pack *A Sense of Place* in the 'See also' section (page 25) provides a large number of photographs of the National Memorial Arboretum which can support reflection and understanding.

Explore with pupils questions such as:

- Why are so many memorials to those who died in war found in places of worship / use religious language and imagery / provide a focus for religious services, e.g. Remembrance Day?

Activity 2
A memorial expressing thankfulness

1 **With the class**, conduct a series of searches on the Commonwealth War Graves Commission website – www.cwgc.org – entering terms such as 'Christian', 'Hindu', 'Muslim', 'Sikh', 'Gurkha'.

   Ask pupils:

   a What do they notice?
   b What surprises them? Why?
   c What questions do they have?

2 **Show pupils** the short video (4.24 mins) 'Forgotten Heroes – The Muslim Contribution' on the EMEL website.

   See: www.emel.com/article?a_id=1699&id=65

   The video commemorates the sacrifice of Muslim soldiers in both the First and Second World Wars.

   Ask pupils to:

   - **discuss** whether this video answers any of their question. Why/why not?
   - **suggest** why some people feel that Hindu, Muslim and Sikh solders are not remembered among the war dead as often as they might be.

3 **Tell pupils** that a Muslim organisation called EMEL ran a campaign to get a consultation process started to design a fitting memorial for Muslims who fought and died in the two world wars.

   Ask pupils to work in small groups to:

   - **design** a fitting memorial to commemorate and celebrate the sacrifice of Muslim soldiers (or Sikh, Hindu and so on) who died in the two world wars.
   - **consider** the religious beliefs and sensitivities of the religion they have chosen and how these affect the design of the memorial
   - **decide** where their memorial should be placed, e.g. a national memorial in a major city; a series of local memorials in towns that sent large numbers of men to the frontline; a permanent exhibition in one of the nation's museums; the National Memorial Arboretum; or somewhere else.
   - **present** their design to the class, giving clear reasons for the design ideas and location for the memorial they chose.

RE Today Services

FOR THE RE SUBJECT LEADER

Exploring thankfulness in the RE curriculum

In general

Thankfulness (or similar concepts such as **gratitude** and **appreciation**) features in most lists or collections of values, whether from religious or non-religious sources.

The activities in this publication enable pupils to explore the beliefs and values connected with thankfulness, and to consider and reflect on the practical implications of expressing these in relation to themselves, others, the community and the world. **This process is central to religious education**.

RE and values education

RE has a key part to play in values education in schools by:

- helping pupils to make the link between belief and behaviour

- supporting spiritual and moral development through reflective exploration of the wisdom of religion and belief traditions and in the teaching of key religious figures

- enabling pupils to consider their own beliefs and values and those of others in the light of their learning in RE.

Many schools take a whole school approach to values education and base their work on one of a series of published resources, such as those mentioned under 'Resources' on this page. Whatever your type of school, and whether or not you formally structure your values education on one of these resources, there is a wealth of useful material for all schools to draw upon to create an appropriate learning environment in which RE can take a lead role.

Resources for values education

1 Christian Values For Schools

Christian Values For Schools presents 15 values from which schools can choose to help them delve deeper into their distinctive character as church schools. The values are: **reverence; wisdom; thankfulness; humility; endurance; service; compassion; trust; peace; forgiveness; friendship; justice; hope; creation; koinonia** (community or fellowship).

Each value is supported with background and theological information, and a set of accompanying questions and cameos (videos, images and text, showing the values in action in the daily life of schools). The resources are free.

See: www.christianvalues4schools.co.uk

2 Values for Life

Values for Life is a resource written by diocesan schools advisers. There are 12 values: **courage; creativity; peace; trust; forgiveness; justice; thankfulness; compassion; friendship; hope; truthfulness; humility.** These are introduced in key acts of collective worship and there are practical suggestions on how to follow this through in the classroom.

Living Values is a complementary resource, full of examples of excellent practice in schools across the UK. It shows how values can underpin every aspect of school life, including: policy development; the whole curriculum; the work of the governing body; and spiritual development. Sample pages are available for download.

See: www.gloucester.anglican.org/resources/jfish

3 Living Values Education Programme

Living Values Education Programme is aimed at providing guiding principles and tools for the development of the whole person, recognising that the individual is comprised of physical, intellectual, emotional and spiritual dimensions. Resources and details of workshops and seminars by trainers to introduce the programme to schools are available.

See: www.livingvalues.net/reference/excellence.html

Activity 1

Keeping a diary of reflection

Ask pupils to:

- **keep a 'Diary of Reflection'** for a day or a week. At the end of the day they should take a few moments to look back and think of all the good things that have happened to them, e.g. people who have helped them, sights and sounds which made them feel good, laughter, friends, family and home. Encourage them to look for the good things, appreciating them rather than letting them slip by.

- **share some of the things** from their diary which they are comfortable sharing with a partner. How many times did they show thankfulness or gratitude to someone as a result of a good thing that happened – and how many times did someone show gratitude to them?

- **reflect on** how often they showed thankfulness or gratitude. Have they 'got it about right' or is a change needed? Pupils set themselves a target to show thankfulness/appreciation more often – and record in their diary what they notice. Does it make a difference? How does it make them feel?

Activity 2

Religious perspectives on thankfulness

Whichever religions your pupils are studying, there will be stories, quotations from sacred texts, poems and music which explore thankfulness/gratitude/appreciation. There are some starting points on this page.

Ask pupils to:

- **invite someone** with a religious faith into their RE lesson to talk with them about what they are thankful for and how they express their thanks in their religious life. Pupils should plan questions to ask, drawing on their learning in RE and their own ideas and experiences.

Buddhism

Let us rise up and be thankful, for if we didn't learn a lot today, at least we learned a little, and if we didn't learn a little, at least we didn't get sick, and if we got sick, at least we didn't die; so, let us all be thankful.

Buddha

Judaism

Be not like those who honour their gods in prosperity and curse them in adversity. In pleasure or pain, give thanks!

Mekilta Exodus, 20:20

Christianity

Finding himself cured, one of them turned back, praising God at the top of his voice, and threw himself at the feet of Jesus and thanked him.

Bible, Luke 17:15–16

Islam

It is God who has made the night for you, that you may rest . . . and the day, as that which helps you see. Truly God is full of grace and bounty to all people, yet most give no thanks. It is God who has made for you the earth as a resting place, and the sky as a canopy, and has given you shape . . . and has provided you sustenance of things pure and good; such is God, your Lord. So give glory to God, the Lord of the Worlds!'

Qur'an, 40: 61, 64

A Buddhist story about thankfulness

In a thicket at the foot of the Himalayan mountains there once lived a parrot, together with many other animals and birds. One day a fire started in the thicket from the friction of bamboos in a strong wind, and the birds and animals were in a state of frightened confusion. The parrot, feeling compassion for their fright and suffering, and wishing to repay the kindness he had received in the bamboo thicket where he could shelter himself, tried to do all he could to save them. He dipped himself in a pond nearby and flew over the fire and shook off the drops of water to extinguish the fire. He repeated this many times with a heart of compassion, out of gratitude to the thicket.

The spirit of kindness and self-sacrifice was noticed by a heavenly being who came down from the sky and said to the parrot, 'You have a gallant mind, but what good do you expect to accomplish by a few drops of water against this great fire?' The parrot answered, 'There is nothing that cannot be accomplished by the spirit of gratitude and self-sacrifice. I will try over and over again and then over in the next life.' The great god was impressed by the parrot's spirit and together they extinguished the fire.

The Teaching of the Buddha

RE Today
Services